THE NEW YORKER

BOOK OF ALL NEW CAT CARTOONS

Also available from Hutchinson
The New Yorker Book of Dog Cartoons

THE
NEW YORKER

BOOK OF ALL NEW CAT CARTOONS

HUTCHINSON
LONDON

© 1998 by the New Yorker Magazine, Inc.

1 3 5 7 9 10 8 6 4 2

This edition first published in 1998 by
Hutchinson

Random House (UK) Limited
20 Vauxhall Bridge Road, London SW1V 2SA

Random House Australia (Pty) Limited
20 Alfred Street, Milsons Point, Sydney,
New South Wales 2061, Australia

Random House New Zealand Limited
18 Poland Road, Glenfield,
Auckland 10, New Zealand

Random House South Africa (Pty) Ltd
Endulini, 5A Jubilee Road,
Parktown 2193, South Africa

A CiP record for this book is available
from the British Library

Papers used by Random House UK Limited are natural,
recyclable products made form wood grown in sustainable
forests. The manufacturing processes conform to the
environmental regulations of the country of origin.

ISBN 0 091 80107 9

Printed and bound in Great Britain by
Butler and Tanner Ltd, Frome, Somerset

THE
NEW YORKER
BOOK OF ALL NEW CAT CARTOONS

"The meaning of life is cats."

"*I tell you, the book has everything—sex, history, consciousness, and cats!*"

DOG DAYS

SYDNEY CARTON REFUSES TO GO TO THE
GUILLOTINE WITHOUT HIS CAT.

"That one is Marvin's __personal__ pussycat."

"*When he leaves, I'm in charge.*"

"Hey, let's do lunch."

"*Just what do you think <u>you're</u> up to?*"

"We're out of flowers."

"I feed the cat nothing but veggies."

"*If you must know, Jimmy, you came from a box in front of the market. It said 'Free Kittens.'*"

"*What is it with you, anyway?*"

"He's my best friend and he works hard all day.
Couldn't you at least wag your tail?"

"*Jeopardy!* is on."

Second thoughts

"We're slapping you with a stress suit, pal!"

"Yeah, I was into the pet thing for a while, but that scene wasn't for me."

27

"You never chase me through back yards anymore."

*"I can't believe it! I had the key right in my paw,
and you had to cough up a hairball!"*

"What the hell was I _supposed_ to do? I've been declawed!"

"*Putty took a wife. Her name was Pussums, and she bore him Little Gentleman, Biddy Boo, Savor Tooth, Fluffy, Harry Cat, and Caesar. Then Little Gentleman begat Little Gentleman II and Friday and Twinkle Toes and Possum Tail and . . .*"

"People are O.K., but I prefer little pieces of string."

"Do you ever miss New York?"

"Samantha is Harry's, but Homer here is mine from a previous marriage."

"He may have found his mittens, but he's lost all sense of propriety."

"As you were."

"Before Prozac, she loathed company."

"We are not amused."

"*Big deal! You're still all bums to me.*"

THE CAT LADY

"All you really need in life is the love of a good cat."

"I'm afraid we'll have to keep him overnight. Are you going to need a loaner?"

WHO'S <u>REALLY</u> RUNNING THE CITY

A LATE ENTRY FOR "POOR RICHARD'S ALMANACK."

"The phrase you're groping for is "Thank you.""

"I need some answers, people."

"Do you, Edward and King, take Susan and Fluffy, to have and to hold . . ."

"*Mom always liked you and Pinkie and Spike and
Custard and Fluffy best.*"

STEINBERG

55

"Dolly—Gregory Strong, author of 'A World History of Cats.'
Need I say more?"

"Honey, I don't want to hide anything from you. I collect
pictures of cats in my spare time."

"I'm going out. Do you need any voles?"

"She's not all over you, but she gets the job done."

"O.K., *just for our records, how many of you have been getting away with sleeping on top of the VCR?*"

How well do you really know your household pets?

NORELDO, THE MENTAL MARVEL, READS THE MIND OF HIS CAT, NED.

"*A wonderful cat is coming into your life.*"

"Sorry, we're all cat people. The dog people are in that boat over there."

"Oh, lots of things were different when I was a child. For one thing,
it wasn't all cats. It was dogs."

"We tried to talk her into coming, but you know how cats are."

"I'm not worried about you, Henley. You'll land on your feet."

1.

2.

5.

6.

68

3.

4.

7.

"*To this day, I can hear my mother's voice—harsh, accusing. 'Lost your mittens? You naughty kittens! Then you shall have no pie!'*"

"Oh yeah? When's the last time <u>you</u> dragged anything in?"

"I have a couple`of other projects I'm excited about."

"It was so depressing. When I go to the theatre, I want to be entertained."

STAR

RATS

STEINBERG

"Curiosity."

*"We had the usual exchange of gifts—she gave me this
diamond collar, and I ate all my dinner."*

*"She turned fourteen years old this week,
but we think she's ageless."*

"*Are we talking about life style or orientation?*"

"Guess who?"

"It's a cat calendar, so it may not be all that accurate."

"*I'll give you three cans of Happy Herds Condensed Milk for two cans of Affaire de Coeur Flaky Salmon.*"

"There's no need for your kitty to be envious. After state and federal taxes and legal and administrative fees, Chessy's share of Aunt Martha's estate came to hardly anything."

"I've been wondering if there isn't some way _we_ could capitalize on the cat craze."

Index of Artists

The text of this book was set in Caslon Old Face No. 2.